AF241579

Recruit to Deny

Recruit to Deny

POEMS

Buffy Shutt

INDOLENT

www.indolentbooks.com
Indolent Books
209 Madison Street
Brooklyn, NY 11216
ISBN: 978-1-945023-37-8

Special thanks to Epic Sponsor Megan Chinburg
for helping to fund the production of this book.

Always For Peter

&

To Calder and Silas

who reintroduced me to the present moment

Everyone has three lives:
a public life, a private life, and a secret life.
GABRIEL GARCÍA MARQUEZ

CONTENTS

ONE

Ballet Class

He corrects her. She torments him
with weight gains, a tiny ring in her nose,
no bra, no panties, no line.
She refuses to spread her legs
in second position grand plié.

Her period has stopped.
Sometimes red drips appear in the crotch
of her pink tights. She smells
the ridges on his fingernails, his white hair.
Touches her so close she cannot exhale.
He works to make her
flat, bony, alert.

Others are better, but she jumps high,
turns like a pinwheel.
He watches her in the mirror.
Strokes his two Russian wolfhounds
dozing at his feet, turns to tear her down,
tears her down, tears her.
She longs for the skinny doe-arms
of the dancers on the shore to glide by
and kiss and stroke her.

She drops back to retie her shoe.
He waves the music off.
His voice jerks her to the center.
The others flatten against the wall,

trail their feet in rosin, tug their leotards
out of the crack in their butts,
drag up their tops, easy cover for flat breasts.
then fall in half,
ostriches.

A solo.
The blister on her heel oozes.
In the changing room, crouched
under a cloud of sweat
she hides M&Ms in her toe shoes.
She takes center. Fifth position. Still.
The piano player will not look at her.
The M&Ms begin to melt.

If he ever invited her
to dance Swan Lake,
if he ever invited her
to understudy in the corps,
never actually getting on stage,
she would stuff her toes shoes with
soft white bread.

Art of the Striptease

You unbutton your baby blue sweater.
Heads pop up, hands tight to their double espressos.
You're presenting the movie's ad campaign.
You pull off your earrings.
Toss one gold hoop to Boss.

He sucks on it; one you let roll down The Table.
The Others jump for it.
Boss and MoneyMan watch.
Rearrange themselves.
The Others dip into their iPhones.

Fingertips on your collarbone,
you lean back, offer a peek-a-boo of blinding white
and their phones fall silent.
Challenge takes its place at The Table.
You know they feel the heat.

You tease off your silky blouse, let it fly,
shimmy down your pants.
You thumb the clicker, run the slides.
You hook your fingers into the top of your panties.
All eyes on you now.

You don't mind their ogling your breasts,
or debating your ass,
your saucy side dishes.

You mind they might see your heart squeezed,
your ribs working overtime to keep yourself stitched together.

The only other woman takes the last thing,
your shoes, places them with respect in the corner.
You stand barefoot. Thong-naked.

You're close, very close to approval.
The air is thin, almost blue
when the meeting is broken.

Hang on.
An actor-director-producer shows up.
Heat-seeking Boss missiles out the door.

Hard to the mirror in a ladies' room
on another floor,
hipbones against the sink,
you dream-hate:
How to Get to The Table.
how to get to the table.

You deserve The Table.
You want to watch someone else,
be deprived of status,
be taken apart,
to strip.

Why Didn't You Quit

when you peed on yourself during endless meeting?

    It was only a few drops,

    and I had put on a maxi pad.

when you had to put on a wetsuit for that meeting on a raft?
In the ocean. Granted it was Malibu.

    I thought he was kidding.

    I liked him.

when the movie star snarked the poster looked like a blow job?

    I was embarrassed. I considered an answer.

    I knew cocaine was afoot. No help was coming.

when the producer pushed you up against the wall,
put his hand inside your blouse?

    I made a joke.

    I was relieved my nipple stayed flat as a quarter.

when your boss asked you: *want to know how I get hard?*

    I was in a business suit. Navy blue.

    I sat still. As stone.

when he hummed out his answer: *I look at my checkbook.*

    I wanted to. I wanted to quit. But more

    I wanted to prove

    I could walk barefoot across hot coals,

    stand on my head,

    endure it in a pretty silence.

Little Fish

Fattened from lunch, eyelids crackback.
Ambition seems a sweaty thing.
I swim out at Columbus Circle.

31 floors up I duck into the bathroom,
pat myself down with soaked paper towels.
I use the whole stack.

At lunch a college friend and I share
two bottles of red wine. I expense them.
Unsure how I will explain this to Boss.

My friend will become so much more
famous than he is today.
But here, in this murky restaurant,
he is only a little ahead of me.

Blinded, on the street,
the sun burns out my envy.
I say I had too much to drink.
I mean, I want to succeed like you.

He hails a cab—blazing yellow—
opens the door; his words float back—
I'm going home. Too hot too drunk
to go back to the office.

Got to get back.

Boss will want to roll calls.

I have scanning to do.

To ease my reentry

I snatch a floaty gift for Boss—

a petite, flinty woman.

I overpay.

Her new scarf sinks to the bottom of my bag.

Female on an Icy Bridge

My kids know the drill.
This daily exchange of prisoners.

Halfway across the bridge, I twist back.
They, better spies,

do not hesitate, do not mouth silent words
or shrug off their heavy backpacks.

My mother called us baby dolls.
She planted a flag in my navel.

She put our blankets in the dryer before bedtime.
Her attention was a sharp thing.

She tempted us with orange sections, with games.
She loves me, she loves me not.

Knotted a rope and lashed herself to us.
I have the rope still,

a thinning piece of string.
I wind it around their wrists and lie down beside them

sucking out their day. My second shift begins.
They run full tilt to me, we spend

a long night making them love this bargain
but diplomatic efforts

break down at dawn and again
we separate on the bridge.

Recruit to Deny

Commit murder. No body. No blood. Many weapons.

Murder the urge to call out when drowned out.

Sever ties with those who call me/us dear and

fondle the collar of my/our blouse with such tender ferocity

I want to surrender. I almost surrender. We surrender.

I pull open the freezer.

Scrounge for ice cubes

to cool my surrender. Fill me with ice water.

Use the secret ice water to

reform

to cool me

to ice me

to let me

Fridging is a term for a storytelling device

that kills or harms a female

character to motivate a male hero.

Camille Claudel, sculptor, Rodin's muse and lover says excuse the dust on my blouse.

Jerri Cobb, recruited to be an astronaut, passes all the tests. They force ice water into her ears. She never goes into space.

Simone de Beauvoir shows Sartre her novel. He holds his nose.

John Bratby paints over his wife, Jean Cooke's canvases when he needs one for himself.

Lightning

She's asked to wear a lid to work.
She pretends it's *a crown.*
To fit, she is tamped down.

The glass is thickish, usually transparent,
can carry colors well: cobalt, amber,
peeled plum.

Now and then, like last Tuesday,
she leaks out,
a pie's innards dripping down
the side of the she-pan.

On Fridays
she unscrews her lid,
tips herself over,
floods the halls,
swims out.

Monday morning, Boss knocks off her crown,
peers in, screw-threads her lid back on.
Her *outerband is reusable.*

Thursday she re-centers her crown,
remembers her mother threw a jar at her,
sailed across the kitchen like a hot foul ball.

Her fingers trickle out, feel around for

the jar's bulging letters,

little nipples spell *Lightning*.

A sealing method. Popular since the 1880s.

Get in.

My first boyfriend was a volunteer fireman and that's all I'll say about him

except

how he lives on the edge

a fast one to come in case the bell rings.

I am in his local jurisdiction,

he went to high school with my sister.

His work is Fire Suppression.

Bent over, a quick poke,

he looks for the start of the fire.

On the hook and ladder,

I sit on his lap, his beauty steers.

I wish I had a cigarette,

bring cool fire to a fire.

I'm afraid of the word condom.

His friend in an ice-blue dress shirt,

dances a skinny joint over a tiny round table.

My sister's laugh floats out over Wisconsin Avenue.

I lay my burning forehead

on the cool narrow railing.

Back home. An exhausted tripwire,

I lounge on the loveseat.

The fireman's friend texts me.

Daddy keeps reading, smoking.

Points at my dirty feet.

But I never left my sister's apartment.

Oh, slipped off my shoes, on her balcony.
He stubs his cigarette into
the square crystal ashtray.
I am that fiery tip, smashed out headfirst.

Before I can explain
we are standing in the hall,
I lunge-flirt with the mirror
an ugly glint with leaves like flames
and we both see

it's not my dirty feet
he's talking about.

What Went Wrong

First, give your children your body.
All of it— your blood, their blood,
your pain, their safety. Greedy,
they take your lungs, your fingernails,

your common sense.
Next, give them your childhood.
They tear at it with baby teeth,
so they can reheat you later.

Then, give them your husband.
Turn him out of your bed, cut him
from the banter. Let bribes and threats
swell the house.

Give them your heart.
Now hyenas, they scavenge along the road.
Something—a longing to sniff their necks,
tiny fingernails so sharp they drew blood—
sees you through these seconds, these years.

Give them your dream.
They swoop in pecking,
cackle the sweetest songs.
Their wings spanning your adult life.

Soon enough give them your death
and they will look down,
mesmerized, by the dark soil,
the dirt, the shifting earth
scrambling to cover you.

The Artist Paints Everything White

He takes off this morning
on a peeling rowboat.
He pushes away from the life we own.

Rounding the black bend in the river,
the banks suddenly high,
he disappears.

I walk barefoot to the kitchen.
One mug. The pantry door is ajar.
I scratch off the red graffiti
with my thumbnail.

Today I will smear paint
into the damp to stop the spread.
To stop the river crossing the floor.

I lift up my arms. A memory of legs apart.
I will stay up all night painting everything white.
He might be here in the morning
like fog.

What I'll Tell Frank O'Hara

Fifth Avenue pushes me around.
Distracted men and determined
women with evening plans
run me over.

My not-important job is blocks behind me
near Columbus Circle where there is

no click of spiked heels,
no flights of gold.
No purse the size of a candy bar.
My building a tall white bullet.

The Seagram Building's all glass and bronze ribs.
Frank, I see your *dropped hot dog, sodden.*

Maybe we'll have lunch there one day—
the fountain, the Rothkos, Picasso's curtain,
the assigned tables. Yep,
New York is greater than the Rocky Mountains.

I said it was green glass, you said whiskey brown.
You put your tongue in my mouth,

jerking your head like you're already
downtown on Tompkins Square
with your friends outside of work.
Over there, that's green. The Lever House.

Seagram is skinned,
set back from the street like a church.

I feel a peculiar wickedness
rise up from
my ankles. I want to be
green marble, stone.

I want to be every window,
every revolving door,

every department store facade,
every bank glass,
every skyscraper's body,
every taxi's windshield.

I force a couple to break hands to pass by,
the woman in all black harrumphing,

the cars' complaining
twisting through rush hour,
the subway rumbling up
through the grate,

your plans, my breath—all travels up the side
of the building and splashes back down

and for a second,
I can't hear anything.

I am dragged to the 5:53.
We share inky fingers pressed
against the afternoon *Post*.
Men five o'clock-shadow flirt.

I dangle on a spandrel,
on that bronze-y mountain's shoulder.

I search for an empty seat.

TWO

Song of the Movies

Through wide doors, the ushers
(boys I've known since middle school) nod me out.
I sing the movies.
I wing back home.
I love movie dialogue, a red lifesaver floating in my mouth.

I love movies so much, that soon enough, when boyfriend is in the door,
I want to mouth off, use my movie-weight to push him around.
He's tired from work, he wants only a joint and a beer.
He runs his hands over me,
makes me spit out the lifesaver.

Movies under my nails, movies clinking in my glass like ice,
thirsty, I have to sip.
At work, I steal my friend to smoke outside and
talk movies movies, movies. Old movies—
one screen in the sixplex makes room on Fridays.
Online I reserve D 105-106.

Friday is coming and I love movies.
Ginger & Fred will soon be gliding over us,
Nora will teach us to martini and wisecrack with Nick.
I will be Claudette Colbert and for two weeks
he will only get to touch me on my left side.
I will grab his hands and shove them into
Kate Hepburn's trouser pockets.

Stop! my friend begs. It's only hump day.
I promise her Friday is coming.
I get shouty and go on about Bette
throwing off her matching fur jacket and hat.
Ingrid gets poisoned for being a spy.
Audrey eats her necklace on Fifth Avenue,
I hope Wilma's a swell girl.

It's the women thirty feet tall we love.
We unbutton our blouses to let their power splash over us.
We wince when their fast-talking-high-heel-clicking-
padded-shoulder-strutting smacks into a wall,
bricked up by some guy.

Tell you what, I'll toss a coin, heads you stay, tails you go
and a fist comes out, the odd gun,
we cover one eye, rear back.

My friend leans in, whispers
never get married. I'm thinking something else—
like how about I grind my big movie-cocktail ring
into his face. I love movies.

I love movies when Friday night arrives, I pull at my friend.
Come with me if you want to live.
The lights take their time dimming,
like a boy leaning in for a first kiss.
The dark snatches us up. Oh, I love

movies. A rage, a rose,
something to squander. Something to savor.

Marilyns

She's dead.
We hear this driving home from church.
My sister kicks her feet against the front seat.
She couldn't care less.
Radioman says suicide.
I am a bird forced to ground.

Daddy says he met her once
in an elevator at the White House.
She whispered to the crowd of three,
I'm not wearing panties.
My mother turns around to announce
Arthur Miller was mean to her.
How does she know this?
Daddy steadies me in the rearview mirror,
don't believe your Mother's Marilyn.

I slam my bedroom door
and twenty Marilyns flutter
against the bang but hold.
Marilyns cut with pinking shears,
Marilyns on hot skirt-lifting nights,
Marilyns in fur and black.
Marilyns with bare shoulders hunched,
lips apart,

surprised.
I lie down, her eyes on me.

My feet press against interlopers.
I never loved anyone who died.
My hands roam my nothing breasts.
I study her steamy *Some Like It Hot* walk.
I jump up—dot a beauty mark on my right cheek,
inhale my trifold vanity mirror,
flop back down.

I carry the Marilyns around for years.
Slipping inside her to interest men,
then mimicking her distrust.
Once I see the beaded gown
she wore for JFK—*no panties*—
and see the shimmer of 2500 crystals,
I set her down.

So tiny, so heavy, so perfect
floating in a Plexiglas box.
Too small for me,
nevertheless, I squeeze my waist.
Happy Birthday, Mr. President.

I Say His Name

once a day under water or inside
a swallow of the hottest coffee
I can stand.

I can spell his name backwards—and forwards
like spinning this dial is my job.
I drag my nails across my arm, the letters of his name visit like ghosts.

Hugging close to the streets he drives down,
sniffing the hot tires finally silent in his driveway,
I track him down. Skulking

in his suburban woods,
I crouch down
start to dig.
Start
to
dig
him
up.

I wipe my hands, pick the fur off my face.
Dig his name out of my dirty fingernails.

Resumé

The best wife I ever was
was when I was fucking you.

For him, I was patient,
his jokes genius,
I made spaghetti Carbonaro.

For you, I was unhinged.
Once I breathed you in,
human rules bled out.
Our end wonderfully surgical,

though I still see you five days a week,
8-10 hours a day.
In the elevator,
reaching for a muffin,
snuffing out my idea in a meeting,
thighs-touching on power points
and talking points,
shaking a client's hand,
your casual text lying in my hand,
face up, making me wait.

Our sex uprooted asphalt,
tore tops off cars,
sheared the sides of buildings.
Our debris taught me how to lie.

I was an animal—

sniffing is too soft a word,

so ladylike it won't get me home.

Disaster Fucking with Bette Davis

Bette Davis (Julie): "But are you fit to go? Lovin' him isn't enough. . . "

Margaret Lindsay (Amy): "I'll make him live or die."

Bette: "It's not a question of provin' your love."

Jezebel

Hands on my nipples—did he wash his hands?

His breath on my neck once a good thing,

now wish he had a mask.

The virus is here. Close by. Possibly in this room,

possibly on the tip of his penis now ramming inside me.

The TV is on.

A Bette Davis movie. Her red dress screams through the black & white.

We usually turn off the TV

but maybe he thinks I will break in two if it goes dark.

I wiggle under him getting comfortable with the idea,

the idea of the virus inside of me. That's okay.

I'll contain it. Somehow.

I leave that and put a slide under the microscope.

My daughter upside-down. I smell citrus. Tangerines.

She likes the ones called cuties.

Think of my daughter,

our daughter, no, my daughter

He goes long stretches without thinking about her.

He isn't thinking about her now as he metes out
some rhythmic present I don't want.
If she gets sick, what will I do?

I can't go to her apartment. I can't tell her that.
I can't tell anyone that.
I'm not strong like BD in *Jezebel*.

I'm more Margaret Lindsay's Amy, saccharine, dull-pretty, mewley.
I mouth the dialogue. Bette's southerness glues my tongue.
Who will save poor feverish Henry Fonda?

The bed is now a bulletin board. I am pinned to it.
He gets imaginative, replaces the televised sport
with a new still-in-Olympics-trial position. I go along.

Gives me time to consider
what a bad mother I am.
And a bad lover.

Now I am on my stomach, half off the bed.
The virus, stealthy and fast, flipped the bed upside-down.
I don't give a shit I am a bad lover—that I can hide.

I am flattened, squeezed into a grain of rice.
I am a bad-mother-grain-of-rice.
A tiny nothing.

He's keeping at it. I hate his body
in perfect harmony with his lust.
He spends long minutes away from the virus.

I wind up inside those tiny, distorted profile pictures
on Instagram of doctors-strangers-brave nobodies.
Pleading. My brain is a firefly.

I am on top now. Not so out of it as I want.
I give a little back to him.
I take him in my mouth.

Nancy Reagan pops into my head. They say she gave great head
in the backseat of limos when she was Nancy Davis,
Just say no, Nancy.

The wife behind the scenes, the husband, out front.
They're responsible for this.
When the air traffic controllers' union was busted,

the dam broke and when it broke
the virus oozed.
Oozing became

dripping. And dripping became streaming,
streaming rushing and rushing flooding
and the virus took hold.

Am I insane fucking while Mommy— what our President
called FLOTUS —floats around in my head?
Get out.

 I can only think if my daughter calls me,
if she calls me, if she calls me,
what if I have to stand up to the virus?

Will I do it?

Am I little deluded Julie? I want to be Bette.

I hear our whole conversation, what my daughter says,

what I say, what she says, what I say.

She is soft, lets the phone slip from her mouth,

refuses FaceTime, won't write down

what I am telling her —

write this down, write this down,

remember this password.

She coughs or clears her throat, calls me Mommy.

Each time we fly close. . . the virus interrupts,

the white rabbit with his fucking ticking pocket watch.

I don't know how long we fuck. He comes.

I'm out. Disaster sleeping.

I am nobody's Mommy.

No Goals Required

She's found the missing bees. They're hiving in her larynx.
The buzzing makes her late for work.
She wonders about the bees while spooning out the honey.
Must spoon it out—every day at one p.m.
Where to put this stickiness?
She sees something online about honey containers on sale,
passes it up and can't find it when she scrolls back.

After work, at work, on the bus, in bed, watching TV,
she plays a left-brain/right-brain game on her phone.
Saturday, she takes a cookie cutter from a box of her mother's things,
slices her stomach. Bits of someone else's world plop onto her lap.

By two a.m. heat floods her—anger a lively companion,
thumps at her toes like a hit of cocaine.
Don't you go giving up that anger, her mother says
as she lays about with the radio—TV—iPhone.

The kid had a gun.
The security guard heard a shot. Waited to go in.
Three mothers— the shooter's, the security guard's, the dead boy's—
are wondering why.

One of them posts on GoFundMe.

Only 30 seconds to set up:

mobile friendly,

no goals required

for a fourteen-year-old boy's funeral.

Deprived of Sleep Brain
May Start To Eat Itself

From a toilet of miscarriage

From silence

From a page of type

From the water/ beach/ drop

in a bird's call

into a man's mouth.

We all wanted older men.

False Spring

Seven birds hold a funeral
in my backyard.
Uninvited, I spy
the mourners dressed in black,
watch their claws grapple
the hymnals of dried grass.

Alert to danger, unraveling—
five keen and two, tight in their grief,
stand apart, sentries nodding to a
shared internal clock.

I hang back.

A wren sings 36 notes a second,
a solo no human can hear.
Two doves swim an arc of grey-white,
a canopy of privacy. And strategy.
Murderers attend the services
of the ones they kill.

I hang back.

The mourners memorize my face
and take turns searing the sky
with the dark blue, the black,
the sketch of red that is

rage and sorrow.

They folk-dance apart

and there in the empty circle

am I.

October
So. Cal

I sit in hot water,
the trees crack their bones.

I smell next door's 10:00 am smoke,
so keen I will buy cigarettes at the 7-Eleven if I go out.

I hear one crow, two, six, losing count.
A mighty conversation, possibly of the fires.

I hear the chainsaw coming across the canyon.
The saw floats inside the tub trimming my bones.

My friend texted it is snowing where she lives.
She is looking at places that are warmer and cheaper, not in America.

Four palm fronds hang upside down.
Discarded witches' brooms left by the Santa Anas.

This hot tub, this backyard, these blades of grass too big.
They are as big as the ocean.

The sun dips me up.
The sun dips me down.

The Drinking Game

Come on, wear the mask to bed!
He looks at me like I'm crazy.

It'll be fun. Sexy. Sex us up.
(I don't say please.) I sway,
letting my tongue hang out
over the mask. My stomach hangs out
—a ten-pound nerve ending—
since March.

The Covid has made my husband
more masculine.
It's the name mostly.
Not soft like saddle shoe or swan.

He reads books on his Kindle.
Masculine books. Woody Allen, Roth, Coates, Mike Nichols,
Bruce, Kendi. Dueling Bellow bios.
At night the Kindle spreads a funnel
of not quite white light.
He follows a tunnel away from me.

I start a drinking game.
The game is simple. Name three people
you admire or wish you were.
Name three people fast. A shot.

With each shot I jerk the glass up,
squeeze men's names
between finger and thumb.
They fly off my tongue, fast gnats
around spoiling fruit.
I wipe my mouth, a wine-dark sea.

He rolls his eyes up to the ceiling
pretending to consider his names.
He's thinking about having sex later.
Slams down a few names. Like mine— all men.

Our kids in another room,
one unemployed, the other a remote truant.
A blue light ghosts out their door.
They sleep all day, up all night.
I've forgotten their names.
Two boys.

Soon I will go out
for organic supplies:
milk, bread, earphones, weed,
and I won't go back.

I'll walk across the country.
I will walk myself young again
and meet (the) women
who will knock my socks off.

Hunger

I eat our marriage for lunch.

I hang our marriage in a birdhouse—dangerously high.

I stuff cotton up my nose to kill the odor of this marriage.

I strangle our marriage by holding my breath.

I hear the marriage-motor turning off, shuddering.

It goes silent.

THREE

The Housewife Reads Yukio Mishima

My mother flings her wedding ring.
It skitters across the polished floor.
    My father sits in the father chair (weekends, after dinner).
    He watches the gold halo fly close to him and then
    veer into the dining room.

My mother says there are worse
things than dying.
    She reads Yukio Mishima novels at night.
    She goes to a spa in a strip mall in mid-afternoon.
    Sits in a small sauna wearing goggles.

My mother never sat in a sauna until she was 35.
    She worked for a lapidarist for three and a half years.
    She has library cards in four different cities.

My mother goes tonight to a spa in a strip mall.
It will close at 8:00PM, in thirty minutes.
    She lies on her stomach in the small sauna,
    the pages of her novel spread out.

Preserved

Mama puts the two girls,
born fourteen months apart,
in a cradle. Blankets them in an embroidered heirloom.

The girls grow smaller. Stiller.
Swaddled, they try out their fingertips.

A boy is born. Interestingly,
he walks all over Mama.
She walks around him.

The girls turn a greenish color.
Using tongs, Mama puts them

on a dish, then in a jar. Paraffins it closed.
They can no longer see each other.
Their tongues peek out like tiny pimentos.

The olive dish is popped into the dishwasher.
Everyone is relieved.

The jar set aside. The air is lighter.
Years later the girls pry open the paraffin.
Shimmy out, they sit (unseen)

six weeks (unshriveling) on the counter
and then they slip into the sink,

past the rubber splash guard, down the drain,
out the pipes. In that last push
before the recycling plant,

they spring loose.

I hate women who say they know exactly when their child was conceived

like they're stenographers recording the act while lying down,
the firing right on target.
It seems a dirty boast.

It bugs me
they want to log this coronation moment.

Where was I exactly
that I didn't notice
the rush, feel the thunderclap's slice?

Now, I'm hanging upside down like
Rembrandt's ox.

My muscles softening. I grow tender.
Suspension transforms my carcass into
an embryo's bonnet.

Don't run out of me.
Envy Mary her notice.

I had none.

Her Status As A Cannibal Is Debated

A new voice thrums through the others.
The tall doctor —adorned with a hard hat—
commands the delivery room.
Wishing it were easy, routine,
charms her into letting his interns observe.
She is as curious as they are.

She wants to reach down
and in
and put her hands over the baby's ears
but they have her miles from her body,

miles from where the baby's head
needs her hands.
Voices strung through a narrow plastic tube
chase inside her.
She tries to ignore the machinery,
the mother-stories of catastrophe.

He pulls. And pulls. The stubborn
placenta seems more important
than the baby. Interns rapt.
She doesn't ask for it,

doesn't plan to bury it, but when
the impeccable doctor, a dribbling
red stain on his coat,
the exhausted interns, that other man,

bending over a clear trolley
stop bothering with her

she reaches down a thousand miles,
tastes it— pennies under her tongue.
A ferric hedge against post-partum.
Mother-stories say freeze it,

it defrosts easily,
fry it up with carrots.
One deep afternoon ransacking the freezer,
she hears a terrorist has taken down
Flight 990 to Cairo killing
her doctor.

Stirring the skillet, she thinks
her baby then
her doctor
now.

We the People Of the Former United States

We, the People of the United States,

Me. You. And y'all.

in Order to form a more perfect Union,

Doesn't have to be perfect.

establish Justice,

See, you can forgive someone masturbating in front of you or let a mom out early for carrying some pot around in her back seat or for creating art about something you know nothing about, appropriating someone else's identity.

insure domestic Tranquility,

Can you stop screaming at me when I accidentally cut you off and what about those statues? Video tranquilizes those shootings in Chicago. Up off your own goddamn knee. Four police officers commit suicide after January 6.

provide for the common defense,

I guess I should buy a gun.

promote the general Welfare,

Good teeth, eighth grade reading level, stock up on that drug that reverses an opioid OD, better homeless tents. Medicate the young crossed-overs. Cages even.

and secure the Blessings of Liberty

I think of my mom here. She had long, wavy hair and big tits. I think you need those to dispense blessings.

to ourselves and our Posterity,

Fuck our grandkids.

do ordain and establish this Constitution for the United States of America.

Amen.

September 17, 1787

Tonight

her arm is a speculum. She spreads the freezer door wide.
Frantic, she paws past furred hot dog buns,
expired spanakopita triangles, looking for
her frozen eggs.

A document appears behind the coffee ice cream.
She snatches her glasses.

Your eggs have been confiscated.
You are requested to appear.
Reclaim Property Department, South Lobby.

Gingerly, she closes the freezer,
feels a gun at her back.
Might vomit, wants to weep.
A painful Kegel bends her over.

Are her eggs face down in a brown attaché case
defrosting, melting, dying?

She listens. *Someone here?*
An odor of blood trails.
These men have the key to her apartment.

She pounds at her phone.

911. 911.

It jumps out of her hand, disappears

under the fridge.

Down on her knees.

Caller, tell me your emergency. . . caller.

On Holiday

Friday, a few more hours.

It will be over.

You'll be three or four pounds heavier,

more coming between the 25th and the 1st.

Then there's his birthday in between.

Not his fault it splashes down in the middle.

One man complains the dog drooled on his chinos.

You laugh out loud, making eye contact with the dog, who nods.

Wait 'til the baby spits up on you.

You promise to sit him far away but

you don't have to worry; he is nowhere near the baby.

The baby who is smarter than he is.

Little genius in a onesie.

That man over there, you might be related to,

is so vacant and big

when he sits down his thighs are

like two platters of dark meat turkey.

When the cold air travels up your sleeves

while throwing out the trash

you want to put rubber bands on your cuffs.

Good gravy how would that look.

The cold keeps you in the house,

but they come over anyway.

You listen, your eyes pinballing around the living room

to the red-haired disappointment,

the grey disappointment, the bald disappointment.

You think about saying some things

in the kitchen while snatching

wine in a plastic tumbler.
You're thirsty to say it, dry, to keep
going you say some political thing like
medical coverage should be better and
eye-nod at your mother's teetering.
But God forbid you steady her, let her knock
over the TV table you push the air aside,
the back of your hand clocks other old ones.
Be you soon, the one with the droopy eyelid.
We aren't socialists.
We stand around, the mothers/wives
hating our husbands our bank accounts
our kids our house
with lint on the carpet
a shower desperate for new grout.
Then you think you could be
happy with any one of them.
Like their hate has put a finger up you,
excited you like maybe there is another
chance once the holidays sift away
you can try out a new you.
Only you know you can't
and if the finger inside wiggles
once more you know you
would follow her anywhere.

Sidelines

Pitching forward

       -May 4 12:24 PM

Kent State came to her in a drowsy call

       -A .45 pistol

her mother's voice saying:

       -29 of 77 guardsmen fire on the students

They should have been in class. Safe there.

       -67 rounds

In the cafeteria they tried to get an exact count.

       -4 dead, one shot in the mouth

Photographed scowling or keeping a secret. Telling everything.

       -20, 19, 20, 20 years old

Touching each other

       -9 injured

something alarming enshrined that day. Some lie.

       - 13 seconds

Miles away, frightened she did not touch the banner they hung over the Admin Bldg.

       -They Can't Kill Us All

though they tried.

       -Four days later 11 students bayonetted at University of New Mexico

The Art of War

Every morning when I get dressed for work
I put a picture of you in my underpants.
By noon you slip, run up to my waistband,
slide down my thigh.
I spend the afternoon,
the commute
the heat
wiggling you back
between my legs.

Gun Show

The Arctic tern
in its lifetime
flies three times the distance from the earth to the moon.

The super-owner
in its lifetime
has between 7 and 140 guns.

This gun owner inherited many of his guns.
He has an "assload of guns."
He will get his 70-year-old mother-in-law a gun for Christmas.

The terns have taken our guns.
Ingenious how they have miniaturized them.
They will take them on their migratory trip.

They will fly 17,000 miles
to drop them in the ocean.
The waves — over-worked —
agree to swallow them.

The terns will land,
strut, bow, their hollow bones on display,
make a nest in the open
and immediately get to mating.
For life.

Here we no longer mate.

Latched to a Glacier

A shot for the pain.
> With dwindling noise and no further fuss,
> they wheel us into a walk-in freezer.
> Sliced out, you weigh down my new mother-chest.

We slide onto a block of ice.
> A slow rocking, ice rattling in a tall glass.
> The pinhole in the sky
> holds us still.

A cormorant flies by
> I am—I am not—I am
> repulsed by the bird's
> say-so.

This erotic rehearsal
> calls me hour after hour.
> I want to lick your milky lips,
> taste what I am making.

Dumped off a thin ribbon of sleep,
> we fall into icy water.
> I let down.
> My legs pant to keep you afloat.

I am a different Shackleton,
> resent the rescue that sits on my lips.

I wait for you,

     insomnia my new snow.

I bend over your head, inhale the earth

     keeping us in orbit.

I am cold, I ache.

       I have never felt freer.

FOUR

Plagiarism

I plagiarize my friend.

I can never locate my own words in time.

I plagiarize hers even when they turn to hot potatoes in my mouth.

I plagiarize her husband and her kids; I steal her Amazon Wishlist,

buy her family gifts—beating her to it.

I plagiarize her slim waist using belts so tight I gag.

And her flirty voice.

Ordering eggs, people want to fuck her.

I plagiarize her pillows, her dishes, her recipes, her garden tubs.

I plagiarize her secrets—strut a bigger life.

I steal all the books she's read.

I plagiarize her eyes,

offer her mine.

In the morning

crows perch in my closet.
A steady row of black T-shirts.

This T-shirt has a thin ribbon around the neck.
Almost fancy enough for a birthday or dinner party.
Who does it think it's kidding?

A panther lives between 12–15 years.
We circle each other.
I taste its frenzy.

This T-shirt has followed me around for years,
rounds up my kids
lays them on the bed beside me.

This one is the night.
I shake it. Signed the papers in it.
Drowned it in wine. Still no answer.

This shirt shouts at me. Its pocket spills with to-do lists.
The last ten pounds.
I wear it three out of four mornings.

This one smells like my best friend.
I rub it behind my ears, on my inner left wrist,
hang it back up. It stays home.

This one is a business sandwich. I parade it. It got me fired.

This T-shirt slapped a guy once

and moved me to the front of the line.

This one I wore to pick out my mother's casket.

A Circling Hawk

Murder's in me
streaking through my body.

Thousands of tiny ball bearings
dancing in
my ballroom.

I have my thumb on it now,
my forearm bulges,
people on the subway don't notice.

Murder
—you think you will never commit—
demands you chase it
away.

Curses, potions, all useless mayhem.
I am close to murder,
work out new names for it.

Office mates, bosses, old lovers,
people in cars, senators
whose names I don't bother to learn

hard to track, need radar, an excel sheet
—my daughter's boyfriend—
I never want to stop.

I never want to stop
until I've murdered all the malarkey,
all the blather.

Murder is pink.
Murder is the mattress
waiting for me when the day is finally over.

Headless In The Garden

The backyard is her body.
A rectangle,
dark-bark limbs,
torso of weeds, nettles, worms.

Her head is not on her shoulders,
in the house, backseat of the car,
on its way to work.

She begs the ants to go
find her head, bring the brainstem.
The ants parading along her spine
refuse.

The sun streams down
nothing to break its fall,
a bee's cloudy wings
beat inside her.

Her fingernails sheets of ice,
platters for her veins,
spleen, lungs, bones, nipples.

Grass replaces her.
Dirt.
Her toes fall
to earth.

The Artist Paints Everything Purple

after William Carlos Williams

I have cut the plums—
purply flesh waits in a large bowl.

   I bring their stones to boil
   stirring occasionally
   let them cool,

      then simmer four more times,
      spoon us out.
      I will be in the jar.
      I left the recipe on the counter.

         Forgive me for scorching the bottom of the pan.

"I Want You To Panic"

Greta Thunberg, activist

Davos 1-25-19

A woman slips out of her coat,

out of her dress,

out of her mother's slip,

her underwear floats away.

She buries her face in the

bath-warm currents

pressing against her chest

and, through a gash,

gills burst out.

She bribes

it all to come back.

The choking coral,

heaving snails,

melting silver balloons of plankton

disappearing under forests.

The silenced infant burbling.

She is losing her grip

and her daughter

doesn't want to have children.

Surprise and Ruin

after Thomas Gray

In one car   a holiday crush to church   the boy rolls his eyes in wonder   at the vast gold and
shimmer   tilts his head to the hymns   unthinking, I hum the chorus   and soon enough
we both tire   skirt out the side door   bumping into cold silver   and stone   and colored glass
we hold hands   my son's son and I   trace the graveyard's gravel paths   he runs ahead   plays
rough with the slabs   I faint a bit at the greyest stone   his unmet relative   mine to know   and
to tell or not   this introduction is hard   hard like the sparkling granite bits just under the
scored name   with a text some might call   holy below the stone angel   she sharpens me
but too late   he's off climbing   one two three   on blocks that announce the dead
the gravestones his ladder   he salutes the clouds   and jumps back down   a rush of him
eyes too big   pants caught in his red sock   rustling in dust   a curled leaf   sticks to his
sweater   and soon enough   he sings a rhyme and pockets a light   blue stone
then flips it to me   I want   to kiss it suck on it   instead settle it on a grave of no one
related   to me to us   exactly   wonder at their rest and soon enough   he flies off, sticking up
the New Year with an empty branch   and soon in a few days   it will all seem glittering

Obits

Reading the obits:

Architect

Scientist

Novelist

Baseball star

Photographer.

I am relieved no important women died yesterday.

Correct for Atmospheric Distortion

The stars will speak again,
they will speak in verse.
The stars are speaking again,
they are speaking in verse.

The telescopes
in Chile, Hawaii, the Canary Islands,
orbit in space—
one with 91 hexagonal mirrors—
see the stars
10 billion light-years away.
They see the stars
10 billion light-years away.

The stars will rewrite the psalms.
They are rewriting the psalms,
rewriting the atoms, the molecules.
All the formulas will be different.

Writing for the first time,
written for the first time,
the rewritten psalms will reach Earth,
100 billion light-years ago.

The stars will speak again
will speak again,
and again.
The rain will be ready.

The stars from billions of years ago
are the stars in the sky tonight.
They come to
fill us up
100 billion years from now.

165

The Bear settles down in my backyard.
The neighborhood text thread unspools.
Many sightings and we, as the oldest couple
on the block, are asked to negotiate
with the Bear. Tonight, at the top of our driveway,
my husband speaks to the Bear.
I hold a can of bear spray behind my back.

My husband and Bear 165 agree
the bears will have the run of the neighborhood
—backyards, streets, pools, playgrounds—
from 6pm to 6am and humans will be free
to roam 6am to 6pm.

165 prefers our backyard and around 5:30,
ignoring the curfew, my husband's disapproval
and the constant text admonishments to not get friendly
with a bear, I go out and share a cocktail with 165.

165 needs water. I dig a primitive watering hole
for him. Takes most of my allotted time
to keep it filled. Against the rules, I dig and fill
all night long. So thirsty, one night he eats
our saggy Halloween pumpkins.

Yesterday he asked me to walk with him
up the mountain not very steep I've been up

there loads of times before the bears
came down. I'll have to explain it to my husband.

I ask 165 for one more day.
I ask for another.
After three months, 165 grabs my hand.
Not aggressive.
I am only a little afraid.

I want to introduce him to my husband,
but my husband would be scared,
would be angry if I tell him
165 has bent over our bed some nights.

I talk. Walk. My words float out, attach
to his fur like snowflakes, meaning melts.
165 says nothing. When I talk about my husband,
he points to rotting leaves and abandoned tree stumps
and the nothing between dead and alive.

Almost to the top I falter, but
he swings back, whooshes me up.
He is a carousel spinning me.
I am on top of the world.
He pulls the brakes, sets me down.

He offers me his paw, dripping
with cool water. I lap it.
I have seen Bear do this many times.
I finger his short fur. Tug at my own.

Big Butt

Poem swings her big butt down the hall,
disappears into the break room.
Poem is the office,

drudgy and dreamy.
Poem carries on three conversations at once.
Poem's got fast fingers, doesn't wear glasses.

Poem ramps up the heartbeat,
overheats the room,
takes over the meeting.

Poem follows me home.
Texts me. Tries to FaceTime.
I don't answer. I'm asleep.

Poem hates me.
Poem bangs on the door, batters the lock,
floats outside the window, spies on me.

At work, I call a window washer to
sway thirty floors up to wipe off
the sex, the message. Poem's breath.

Poem shows up unannounced,
crowding into my cube. I offer Poem
coffee, decaf, chai tea, a double espresso.

I can't tell the difference

between Poem and my desk,

between Poem and the fluorescent lights,

between Poem and the keyboard,

between Poem and my breath.

acknowledgments

Boundless thanks to my mother.
She threw her wedding ring at my father.
I picked it up and ate it.
I acknowledge that I want a ring too big to swallow.

A deep bow to my ballet teacher, Mr. Popov.
He introduced me to an eating disorder.

Thanks to the doctor who refused to refill my Adderall scrip
even after I showed her 500 pages of my manuscript.

Big thanks to the IUD. And to the depression-inducing
birth control pills Planned Parenthood gave me
(almost) for free.

I am indebted to Chase Card Services
for their credit card with its ten-thousand-dollar limit.

Heartfelt thanks to my sister for calling me a cherry blossom.
Its five ruffled petals are a tender pink slip under my clothes.

Thank you, many Bosses for the lessons in pending rage,
weak-kneed ambition and desperate cocktails.

Thanks to the R-rated movies inside me,
the sexy swaggering shoulders—men's and the women's,
the breeze of 24 frames a second.

Thanks to those who made me think I was that good, that I could be on the team.

Applause for your sleight of hand: recruit to deny.

Big thanks for inviting me to join the one party

that agrees not to hold the other party responsible for any danger.

Special thanks to the University of Husband.

And lastly, I want to acknowledge myself

for wearing panties two days in a row,

for coming so hard I got cramps,

for using plastics blindly,

for endlessly grieving over

what I meant to say,

how I meant to act,

what I threw away.

NOTES

"acknowledgments" references the hold harmless agreement; this clause
is used as a release of liability in a contract that protects one party from
injury or property damage caused by another party.

"Correct For Atmospheric Distortion" Atmospheric distortion is the blurring
of an image due to the layer of gases surrounding the surface of Earth.
As starlight travels through the atmosphere, pockets of air act like little
lenses and bend the light in unpredictable ways. This distortion causes
stars to appear to twinkle.

"Disaster Fucking with Bette Davis" quotes from the 1938 Warner Bros.
movie *Jezebel*.

"Marilyns" references Ms. Monroe singing happy birthday to President
Kennedy at New York's Madison Square Garden for his 45th birthday
May 19, 1962. Ms. Monroe died 2 ½ months later.

Recruit to Deny: Many colleges reach out to prospective applicants with
recruiting material, creating false hope that they will be admitted, when
the college only values them as filler for the denominator. The more
students who are denied and the fewer who are accepted makes the
college seem elite. This practice is known as "recruit to deny." Also, a
practice used by some corporations.

"Song of the Movies" quotes from the following movies: *The Best Years
of Our Lives, Only Angels Have Wings, Terminator 2* and references
Breakfast at Tiffany's, The Thin Man, Holiday, Notorious and *Dark
Victory.*

"The Housewife Reads Yukio Mishima." Yukio Mishima was a Japanese
author, poet, playwright, actor and considered by many to be one of the
most important Japanese authors of the 20th century.

"What I'll Tell Frank O'Hara" quotes from O'Hara's 1969 poem "Walking."

I would like to thank

The editors and the editorial and design teams at the following publications where some of these poems first appeared, sometimes in earlier forms: *Anthropocene, Burnt Pine, Califragile, Dodging the Rain, Lumina, Passengers Journal, Riddled with Arrows, River Heron Review, Sonic Boom, The Ekphrastic Review, What Rough Beast, Whatever Keeps the Lights On.*

Kate Klimo, my first reader, college roommate and dazzling best friend. We co-wrote our senior year thesis (The revolutions of 1848) and it ignited a life-long friendship and two co-authored books.

Elline Lipkin, a wonderful poet and my mentor, for teaching me about poetry and revision, and for believing late in the game I could be a poet.

Michael Broder for believing these poems were a book and for making them better at every turn. Adam Bohannon for designing a beautiful cover and a beautiful book.

Katie, Chike, Jonah and Marion: Thursday Poetry Group. You are amazing poets, and without your friendship, insights and encouragement, this collection wouldn't exist.

Laurie and Ken for letting me bring poetry to a prose writing group.

My friends and family who support, love, and inspire me every day: Peter; my kids Jesse & Daisy; my darling big sister Gogo; Katrina; Kathy, my West Coast Best Friend; Topper, best brother, Alison, Bruce, Donna, Jeff, Molly, Katherine, Alan, Judy, Marsha, Edite, my nieces and nephew, and my gurus Nina and Lauren.

ABOUT THE AUTHOR

Buffy Shutt is the author of *Memos from the ~~20th~~ 21st Century* (Bottlecap Press, 2024), a chapbook of poems disguised as corporate memos, and the chapbook *animal magnetism* (Yavanika Press, 2024). A two-time Pushcart and Best of the Net nominee, Shutt's poems have appeared in *Anthropocene, Paper Dragon, Sonic Boom, Door is a Jar, Dodging the Rain, Book of Matches,* and *Split Lip Magazine*, among others. A graduate of Sarah Lawrence College, she spent 30 years as a Hollywood marketing executive working on features and documentaries. *Recruit to Deny* is her debut full-length poetry collection.

ABOUT INDOLENT BOOKS

Founded in 2015 as a home for poets over 50 without a first book, Indolent Books today publishes innovative, provocative, and risky books by a diverse and inclusive range of writers across genres.